Pillow Thoughts

Pillow Thoughts

Courtney Peppernell

Andrews McMeel
PUBLISHING®

"As song writers, poetry has always played a special role in our lives. We discovered *Pillow Thoughts*, and it has been one of the most enjoyable books we have read in a long time!"
—The Chainsmokers

Acknowledgments

A special thanks to the following people and institutions:

James De'Bono
Emma Batting
Patty Rice
Ryan Gerber
Kirsty Melville
Andrews McMeel Publishing
My family
My partner, Rhian

Without each of you, this poetry collection
would not have been possible!

Twitter: @CourtPeppernell
Instagram: @itsonlyyforever
Email: courtney@pepperbooks.org

Before we begin, I'd like to share a story.
Once upon a time there was a jellyfish. We'll call it
You.
You became lost sometimes
You could be a little unsure
You tried very hard
But sometimes it didn't feel like enough.
I hate to spoil the ending
But You is fine
You is still here
You is going to make it.

For Rhian

Table of Thoughts

If you are dreaming of someone

Flowers on Your Doorstep

You deserve flowers on your doorstep
and coffee in the morning.
You deserve notes left on your dashboard
and ice cream sundaes at 3 a.m.
You deserve honesty every day
and to be kissed every hour.
You deserve to be reminded
how beautiful you are.
And if you let me,
I'll show you every day.
I promise.

I thought about kissing you today
and yesterday
and the day before that.
I know I'll think about kissing you
tomorrow
and the day after that
and some more days after those days.
I think about kissing you
slowly
and tracing my fingers along
your lips.
I think about kissing you
in your car, in the rain, on your doorstep.
I think about kissing your
dimple, your cheek, your spot.
I think about kissing only you
not anyone else
just you.

I have been a little off balance since the day I met you. This is because I had never known what it is like to be perfectly aligned.

I think that if you let me,
I'd treat you like the sky.
I'd join up all your insecurities,
bundle all your flaws
into a new constellation,
and search for it endlessly.
I know you don't see yourself
the way I see you
and you still argue
when I call you beautiful.
But all the things you can't stand
about yourself
are all the things I can't
go a day without.
I think if you let me,
I'd build an observatory
just to show you
that all the stars in the universe
will never shine as brightly
as you.

If I loved you, then you'd become my balloon. I'd tie your string to my finger, and I'd never let you float away. Until one day, when you wanted, we'd float away together.

We should kiss.
Not because you passed my way by chance
but because you stopped
and I haven't been the same since.

I never expected you to get under my skin, but now your name runs through my veins and I can't help but let every part of you in.

You're covered in all these broken promises
from people who said they would never leave.
Sometimes afraid of your own skin
and the scars that run deep in your veins.
Are you ready
Are you ready
for someone who could turn you inside out?
No one dares to peel back all the layers of your skin
All this damage,
you're a mess.
Are you ready
Are you ready
Because I want your damaged skin.

This is me.
I am the eye of the storm and my heart is a little broken.
But if you want me, I'm yours.

I am in awe of even the way you walk, and yet you walk right past me.

But what else am I supposed to do
when your hair is soft and your eyes are blue?
And my heart turns over at the sound of your name
only you smile at me the way friends usually do.
I am more of a mess than a rainy day
because you have no idea I feel this way.

The aches in my arms still surprise me, even years after letting you go.

You are the freckle on my nose and I am the freckle on my back. We share the same space but we will never be together.

I swore I would never be happy again the day you said, "Let's just be friends." But the world goes on even when lovers go their separate ways. So I will carry on in the hopes I'll find another lover someday.

Your heart is the sun and its gravity
Pulls me closer to you each day.
But the sun destroys all that it touches;
At least this is what they say.

Life is too short for games unless it's a game of cards.

Don't text back right away; if you like them, pretend you don't;

and don't you dare say I love you first.

Well screw all that.

I will text you back in three seconds; I will tell you that I like

you; and if I love you, I'll tell you every chance I get.

Life is unpredictable, and I'd rather play every card as honestly

as I can than have a deck full of regrets and what-ifs.

Often I wonder
what it may take for someone's heart to grow cold
and I think perhaps the reason is because
their heart was left out in the rain.
And so on rainy days I struggle
because I still don't know how to convince you
that I will be outside in the storm
with an umbrella just big enough
to cover your heart.

A Mulberry Tree and a Park Bench

There is a mulberry tree and a park bench. I sit with a flower in my lap and watch as you pretend not to notice me. Some days you sit next to me on the park bench and you inch closer, and we both blush at the chance of meeting again. But here we are on the park bench with the mulberry tree all because you did notice me.

We don't speak with words.

We speak with a gentle brushing of shoulders, a look across the room, a door opened, a smile as we pass each other, a racing heart as I see you coming up the driveway.

There is power in silence,

and while we don't say a word,

we both know we only want each other.

We cannot all be artists
and I must admit I do not know how to paint
But if I were to take a palette
all my colors would be of you

If you are in love

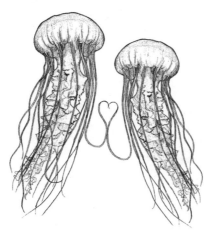

You remind me of home,
of all the simple things in life,
of light and love and the reasons I am not alone.
You remind me of hope,
of the sea and the sky,
every hug and every kiss from your lips to your thighs.
I have flown around the world and met no one like you
because you are all the things I keep coming back to.

Love is not always roses, honey, and tea. Sometimes it is difficult being you, and sometimes it is difficult being me. And in the night if we are restless and our love struggles to make sense, know that I will fight for us. Because I love you, and I know that you love me.

They say don't fall in love with writers
because their poems
are messy
and their letters
are empty words
dressed up to look pretty.
But I say
fall in love with me
because underneath the mess
and in between the lines
is a heart too full of love
that would follow you to any city.

Darling,
kiss me like you need
to feel safe
Because my lips want to know
all the places
you have been hurt
So they can make all the pain
drift away

If I were to build a house
I'd have your arms as the walls
Your eyes as the windows
Your smile as the front door
Your heart as the fireplace
And your soul as my light
And in this house
I'd place my faith
Knowing I'd finally
Found a home

You know sometimes it's the little details
that take up the most room in your heart.
How nervous they get
when you tell them you think they're beautiful,
the way they laugh
even if it's not supposed to be funny,
the way they reach for you and they find you through the dark
even if their eyes are
closed.

There are things I cannot control
and memories I can never erase,
and in the times I don't feel whole,
I will always search for your face.
You are every star burning in the sky,
you are every golden leaf in the tallest tree,
you are a pattern, a snowflake, and every firefly,
and I will still love you even when we're eighty-three.
I will stand by you in every new day
even when people seem so unkind
because you are beautiful despite what they say
and you are everything I've wanted to find.
For all the places in which we go
for one day you might be my wife,
I think we both already know
I am yours in every life.

Love,
I know in my heart without a doubt
even if I can never find the words to say.
You are the one I am crazy about;
you are the one I fall for every day.
When everything doesn't feel right,
I look at you
my sun, my moon, the morning light,
my happiness when all is blue.
With you I am always safe
and every day you make my heart race.
You are my home, my friend,
my saving grace.

Kissing you feels like the start of a new season, the sun in the early morning, and moonlight reflecting on the ocean. There is never a moment that I don't think about your lips and how they make me feel when they are on mine.

If you are in love and the love is returned, be grateful. Because if you take love for granted, it will be overturned.

I was lying beside you
and you had this half smile
because my hands
were drifting down your spine.
And you looked at me
and I lost track of everything.
Because I realized
just how badly
I want under your skin.

I wrote this thinking about you
and how if you were a novel,
you'd be an adventure of sadness and happiness
and love lost in between.
You would remind me of the sky and mountains
and constellations and caffeine.
You would be full of pages
that make me laugh and other times fall apart.
You would smell like history with a worn-out spine
and ink that could still bleed.
You would always be the novel
I took down from the shelf to read.

I like to dream about mirrors,
That there is a mirror world somewhere
A little like ours but different at the same time
And you and I are different
But we are together.
I like to believe whatever world we are in
We are in love
And together.

Of all the maps in the world, the only one I will follow is the map to your heart.

I had a dream that I was under my skin,
lost and wandering around my body.
And in my mind there were pictures hanging on the wall,
and they were of all the people I had ever loved.
But in my heart there was only one picture frame,
and it took up nearly every space.
A single frame,
of you.

People should fall in love more. Fall in love with the way your coffee swirls as soon as you pour the milk in. Fall in love with the look your dog gives you when you wake up. Fall in love with the rare moment when your cat doesn't ignore you. Fall in love with the person who tells you to have a good day. Fall in love with the waiter who gives you extra chili fries. Fall in love with sweaters in winter and cold lemonade in summer. Fall in love with the moment your head hits the pillow. Fall in love with talking to someone until 4 a.m. Fall in love with the days you can hit the snooze button over and over again. Fall in love when a lover stares at you for five hours. Fall in love with the stars when they look at you. Fall in love with the sound of someone breathing. Fall in love with the bus if it's on time or the train if it comes early. Fall in love with everything possible.

And if the moon could talk
I wonder if he would tell the night
Just how lovely she is
With all those stars shining bright

The world still has much love to give, and I see it; I hope that those blinded by hate and rage will feel it. A love so fiery it becomes the color of cherries, and candles, and lipstick, and they will finally see the world with all its love to give.

I will love you even if we don't end up together. Even if you walk away from me, I will still love you. I will love you even if you marry someone else and on the coldest days of the year you spend your nights wishing you had married me after all, because no one knows how to ignite the fire in your soul quite the way I do.

Love makes us both happy and sad, and there is not a soul
alive that has been able to understand why.

When you take a lover who uncovers all your flaws, listens to the very essence of who you are, and embraces you rather than judges you, hold on to this love for a lifetime, as you will never find a love quite as pure.

But the world is exhausted, and the only wealth we have left is love.

It will catch you off guard one day. You'll be so surprised by it you may even lose your concentration. One moment you are living idly by and the next they are on your mind nearly every moment. You'll lose sleep over the next time you'll hear their voice. You might even find yourself daydreaming about a future together. One day you are ordering coffee every morning and the next you can't even order coffee without thinking about ordering theirs too.

You remind me that my heart is still alive
Because every time you come home
it beats so hard
it brings me back to life

It's the last day of the year
and I still lose myself
in good books
and warm tea,
those quiet nights
and writing your name
on my windshield.

What Makes Me Smile

You
in the morning light
after making love
all night.

I hope you find someone who never makes you question your own self-worth. I hope you find someone who chases your happiness as much as their own. I hope you find someone who supports you in the things you are passionate about. I hope you find someone whom you can laugh with and sit in silence with and share your deepest secrets with. I hope you find someone who is your lover, your partner, and your friend. I hope you find someone who treats you as their equal, who learns and grows with you and beside you. I hope you find someone who appreciates all the tiny details that make up who you are. I hope you find someone who respects your heart, your family, and your values. I hope you find someone who reminds you that you deserve the love you give.

If you are heartbroken

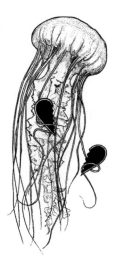

I tried to stop loving you
so I built walls around my heart
and found other names
to whisper in the night.
But you carved yourself into my veins
whether you meant to or not.
And sometimes I wonder
if you remember the way we looked at each other
or maybe you just forgot.

Perhaps it's just easier to smile and pretend everything is fine, rather than admit my heart's a little swollen from losing something that wasn't even mine.

You told me that I was your rose, but in the winter you turned your attention to all the other flowers in the garden instead of tending to my fallen petals.

My heart is not in my body;
it's lying under the castle you burned down.
Yet I am still here,
an empty shell with bloodshot eyes
and a fake smile.

Sometimes I wonder of all the goodbyes you've ever said
if mine is the one you can't get out of your head.

in the end
we
as in you and me
were never
meant to be

You didn't have to say anything that night; you did everything with your body and your eyes. The way you sat next to me, you were close enough to reach but too far to touch. And your eyes, those eyes that once said you'd love me forever, now spilled tears that this wasn't worth the fight anymore.

When did you become so tired of us?

Don't date broken girls,
my mother said.
"But they deserve to be loved too."
And so I loved a broken girl more than anything;
I just didn't realize she would break me too.

And I count all the days
you say I love you
and I die on the days
you don't.
Thinking maybe you might leave
and praying that you won't.

I never really knew how much the heart breaks
until I was lying next to you
and you were thinking about someone else

I still feel the aches you left behind, even after all the time you have been gone. This heart of mine has been broken before, but this emptiness has never left me quite as sore.

You betrayed me
Then you asked
"Where are you now?"
But how could I stay
When you betrayed me?

It hurts a little and sometimes a lot
when you care about someone
but you're both kind of messy
and the timing is all wrong
and you don't feel like
kissing someone else
but you can't force what's not
and letting someone in
is scary enough
but even scarier
when your heart
isn't as strong.

I picked up all your things
and I put them in a box.
I was going to send them back to you,
all those things you gave me
when you promised I was the only thing you needed.
And then I realized
I can't put every kiss in the box
or return every "I love you."
I can't return every time I held you
or unwrite every love letter I wrote you.
I can't undo every time I touched you
or unhear the way you said my name.
I can't send back every "You're beautiful"
because things will never be the same.
What am I going to do with all these things
if I can never pack them away?

I loved what we had too.
The only difference was that I saw it as
forever
and you saw it as
just for now.

I asked you to ride shotgun with me.
I didn't say hold the shotgun to my heart and
pull the trigger.

It's been a while now and I still miss the way she said my name. I didn't know my bones could ache forever for so long.

They say there's beauty in sadness but I don't think so (at least not like this).

When it's 3 a.m. and alcohol is the only thing that helps me sleep.

They didn't warn me that heartache doesn't always have someone to blame. Sometimes it's no one's fault (it's probably all mine).

I found her sweater the other day and it still smells like her and that spring we spent telling each other we'd be forever.

I didn't really think about how forever could end.

She used to call me beautiful and look at me with eyes that meant it. Now I just don't know how I'm supposed to hear that word from anyone else.

I'm caught somewhere between moving on and holding on and not knowing which one I can handle best.

I feel messy and uneasy and I don't understand how one person with pretty eyes can destroy an empire inside me just by walking away.

Her lips tasted like air after rain and these days all I do is think about the way they felt between my thighs.

My pillow isn't her and the song on the radio isn't ours. I sit next to a girl in class but we can't talk for hours.

Where do I go when a lover and a friend becomes a memory and a dead end?

I saw her by the escalators last week. I smiled at her and she looked the other way. I felt my heart splinter all over again.

Sometimes I write her letters thinking maybe she'll write back.
She never does.

All your senses are heightened when you are heartbroken.
You hear things more clearly because it's better than listening to the drum of your heart.
You feel the sun and the air on your skin because you are trying to feel things instead of shutting down.
You smell their perfume everywhere.
You still feel their fingers as though they are knotted through yours and it makes you cry.

Ghost

It happens. They forget the sound of your voice, the shape of your eyes, and the curve of your smile. When you left, you tried to leave traces of yourself behind. But your smell on their sweater eventually fades, and your things in their drawers get pushed to the back, and suddenly you aren't real anymore. So you are replaced with someone who is. You are a ghost, a shadow, only a memory. So much that you wonder if you even existed to them at all.

You spend your whole life convincing yourself you are a chapter worth following, and then someone comes along and doesn't want to read the ending, and suddenly the whole story falls apart.

That's what happens
when your heart breaks
you tell yourself no one
will ever be allowed inside again
but then someone comes along
with light in their eyes
and suddenly your heart
goes to war with your head

When the stars ask you what it is you want,
why do you speak of a love that tears you apart?
Why do you crave a love that will break your heart?
Your soul is never beyond repair, so stay humble and be kind
and eventually a love will come along
and remind you of why you are alive.

I forgave you for myself.
Not for you.
You were too selfish for me.
So when you broke my heart,
I decided to be selfish too.
Selfish in the way I stopped
Making everything about you.

When you are wounded, sometimes it's best to retreat and heal. But do not stay hidden for too long, because all wounds need air.

Stop trying
to convince yourself
of the things
you already know.
Your head wants
another war
when your heart
needs to let go.

I know what it feels like
for my heart to ache
and my soul to cry.
I know what it feels like
for things to be so hard
it takes everything to get by.
I know what it feels like
when nothing seems steady
and for things to derail.
I know what it feels like
to have person after person
cause your heart to fail.
But one day I hope you see
the love you give yourself
heals all parts eventually.
Until finally she walks in
and sets your heart free
and reminds you why
everyone else
wasn't meant to be.

Breathe in, breathe out slowly, and count to ten. There is no rule book on how to cope when these things end. You may not feel it now, but things will get better, even if life doesn't tell you when.

That's the thing about moving on. You are never going to find a love quite like the one before. The key is to stop wanting the same things and embrace the things to come.

But you have to lay it to rest now. There is no point trying to revive a flame that has long extinguished. You sit at the gravestone of a fire that died out, and yet there is a city of flames burning in the distance. There is no need to punish yourself; you keep this up and you'll be missing out.

If you are lonely

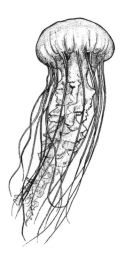

How does loneliness still exist with all these souls in the world?

I fall a little in love
With people who feel so alone
Until the crowd falls away
And they see you
Standing there
Waiting
Like you promised
And suddenly they realize
They're not

My therapist asked, "How do you prepare for the day?"
And I replied, "I count my lies, find my mask, and pretend it isn't easier to fly away."

I am no more the person that you left than you are the person
I miss.

Anchor

An anchor holds me down. I am a lonely ship and this weight will not let me go. I long to be free, to sail the ocean as far as one man can see. But there is an anchor, and the anchor is forcing me to drown.

she's the type of girl
that has a place in her heart
for all the lonely people to go
with their forgotten footprints
in the snow

You are a lonely sailboat, afraid of drowning where no one will see. Yet you forget you have never been alone, not while you have the sea.

Lately I have been making too many excuses
You were a star I caught while gazing, but you burned a hole
in my hand
You stripped me of all my certainty and left me with all these
bruises
You stole so much of me, more than I had ever planned
But it is a new day and I feel like coming home
Back to all the parts of me I'd forgotten, the part that I don't
feel
So alone

But solitude can be a dangerous thing. All that comfort found lost in your own thoughts. It is easy to stay and never return but braver to walk through the tunnel and out the other side.

Imagine yourself a solar system and the sun is your core. You are never going to truly lose the sun. But night does happen, so recharge and be ready to rise again in the morning.

I get jealous
even when people
aren't mine
because others
are reckless
with their hearts
and forget to
be kind

The Bus Stop

There is a bus stop on the corner and each morning a gentleman sits. He feeds crumbs to the birds and whistles a song I do not know. And I wonder if anyone leaves roses on his windowsill to remind him that he is not alone.

I know there isn't a thing
I could say
to make the thoughts in your head
any easier
but I hope you know
that above all the things
running through your head
sometimes it's about
what runs in your heart instead
and if there's anything I know
about the things inside
your heart
it's that they are beautiful things
and strong things
and things that will always
be okay
and if the things in your head
seem a little messy
and the things in your heart
weigh a little heavy
just know that you'll beat
all of these things
and I'll always love you
even with all your things

Sometimes a certain sadness
comes along
and you might not know
where it is that you belong
but your heart is home
and I want you to know
you are never alone.
Sometimes others say
hurtful things
that make you feel
like your face is twisted
and they suffocate your heart
and some days it seems
like everything is slowly
falling apart.
Sometimes your body aches
and you feel like lead
and it's easier to pull your covers
all the way over your head
and pray that you never
wake up
but it's very important
that you do.
So if you don't feel beautiful
when you open your eyes
I hope this reminds you
that I think you are.
Just try to remember this too

In the moments you feel alone
and every mountain is too great
for all the answers left unknown
and convinced it is always too late.
There is happiness in this lifetime
one day these troubles will fade
all your strength is in the skyline
no matter how heavy your heart weighs.
And some days it seems
hope and despair take turns
but despite all our sadness
the sun always returns.

I just wanted you to know
That I'll never care
How far you push me away
Because when I told you
That I would stay
I meant it
You're a little lost
And a little damaged
But you're not hopeless
I know who you are
I love who you are
And that's why I'll stay
So you learn to love
Yourself too

I know you're scared right now
Maybe you miss
Someone
Maybe your heart hurts a little
Or a lot
Or maybe you're not quite sure
Of who you are
Or what you want
But that feeling you
Want back
The one where it doesn't seem
Like the whole world is against
You
It's still here
It never really left
And one day you will realize
That the only person
Who can find it again
Is you

There are little pieces of happiness and they are scattered through your day. So take a basket with you as you step outside, fill it up with all the little pieces, and bring it back inside. Take a moment, just by yourself, take out all of the pieces, and place them on your shelf.

I hope you know you are loved. I hope things get simpler for you, peaceful. Spend your days with easy breaths and soft words. You deserve light through your windowsill. I hope it comes your way soon.

If you are sad

Who made you feel this way?
Like your heart's too heavy
And all its soft parts
Are gone?
Who made you feel
Like this toxic thing
Like no one
Wants you
And you don't belong?
Who made you feel
Like your scars
Aren't beautiful
And your baggage
Isn't worth carrying?
Who made you feel
Like you don't
Deserve everything
And you aren't
Someone worth keeping?
Just tell me where
It all went wrong
So I can make you feel
Like you really belong

You're beautiful
without even trying
but each time
I bring you a flower
it ends up dying
and you don't see
how I look at you
you just keep crying
and the saddest part
is that you're so special
but you think I'm lying

The stars have died
And left their light to you
Remember this when
You feel weak
And worthless
And blue

I have never known what this sadness feels like
when you cannot feel the sun or the air around you
And time they say will heal you
but even my own mother doesn't know what to do.
You said you wouldn't hurt me
You promised to keep me safe
You knew what the others had done
and I fell for the sincerity in your face.
Maybe I deserved this
for trusting someone who could manipulate so easily.
Maybe I deserved this
for not listening when mother knows best.
But all I was trying to do
was show you that even a monster can be loved.

Is that why you play the music so loud? A beat to drown out the thoughts, sound so high you cannot think, lyrics so close to home you don't even blink.

It's exhausting to be locked in your head with all these thoughts that tie you down. Just for one moment, try with all your might to let go of all the things that stop you from being you.

I understand why people take flight from bridges,
I understand why a girl holds a blade to her wrist,
I understand why a grown man cries counting all his lists.
What I wish for the world to understand
is that in these fragile moments,
patience and love are needed most.

My soul is numb, and I am desperate to feel. In times of distress and sadness, mornings are no longer forgivable, and waking up isn't ideal.

I knew what I was going to say; I had rehearsed my goodbye over and over again, but you left without a word.

I keep wondering
how sad do I have to be
for someone to stop insisting
everything is going to be fine?

You promised you would never take a road that I could not follow, yet here we are; I'm crying on the bathroom floor and you've taken the road I couldn't follow.

If I had a list of all the things that still make me cry, some days you would be at the end and others at the very start.

This sadness that they say can be beautiful, what sadness is this? Because my sadness rips me apart from the inside and there isn't a thing beautiful about it.

Of all the tragedies on this earth, there is none more tragic than a person who cannot see their worth.

Sometimes sadness does not have a source. There is no immediate solution, no escape plan from its clutches. Instead, you learn to coincide, as though sadness is an old friend who needs a gentle nudge in the right direction.

The tragedy of what could have been
is nearly as crippling as what once was
but can never be again.

Even sadness needs someone in its corner.

You won't remember, they say, when someone drifts away. One minute you are talking about life's greatest adventures and listening to mixtapes on Monday afternoons, and the next their presence is replaced with silence: a fragile nonexistence with nothing else to lose. But I will always remember our drift. It took up all this space, like a planet with many moons. It was the year you forgot my birthday.

Everyone has a part inside
that aches with a sadness
sometimes you cannot hide.

It will start with the big things, like their seat next to you at the family dinner table on Sunday evenings or their name next to yours on invitations. And then suddenly all the little things will fade too. You won't remember the sound of their voice in the morning or how their hand felt in yours. You won't remember all the tiny details of every date you had or all the conversations you shared late at night. And then one day someone will ask you their favorite color, and you'll hesitate.

There are days where triggers are around every corner, lurking in shadows where darkness spills heavy breaths and tight chests. Anxiety is a devastating thing. No matter how many times you are told to "breathe," it feels as though the air has all but thinned, and despite every logical reason to remain calm, you feel like a ship without its sails in the middle of a raging storm.

Have this framed as a quote in your office one day.

Even if your sadness
feels quite heavy
the truth is
it's just a paperweight
Learn to turn the page

I saw an angel once
But she had lost her wings
I saw an angel once
She seemed broken of all things
I saw an angel once
And asked her why she was sad
The angel looked at me and said
"Because the world has gone mad"

May your weapon be kindness
Your shield compassion
May the flowers grow again
To sprout love from all this sadness

One day you are going to look at someone and say,
"I survived."
There is great satisfaction in that. Even more if the person
staring back comes from your mirror.

If you are missing someone

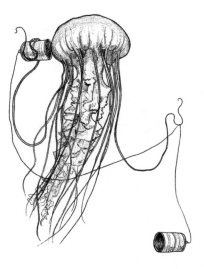

If I had any say and my life to do again, I'd have moved us closer.

There goes the love of my life
Passing by in my dreams
It's been so long since I've knocked on her door
Sometimes I wonder how I will stay strong
And I can't sleep
And I can't think
And I will keep driving this long road
Until the darkness fades and the morning rises
Only thirty more days and lonely nights in between
Until I see her again
It's been so hard
Some days I can't wake up
Some days I fall apart
But she has never left my dreams
There goes the love of my life

We are standing at the edge of the world and yet we still do not meet. You are soaked in daylight and I am covered in the night. My heart yearns for our eclipse.

I am sorry we are in different states and towns
I am sorry for that day I didn't reply so you drove sixteen hours
of dark highway
We are breaking the whole world's heart, all these lonely nights
without each other
Or maybe the world is slowly breaking us
I'm sorry for all the days we've spent separately
I'm sorry for all the time we cannot make up
I'm sorry for being caught up in all your lonely
I just wanted a place to stay

You were always miles away. Maybe you were just always meant to be miles away. The distance saw us together in a dream and thought we were better off without all the mess.

It's 3 a.m. and I am lying alone
Because you just hung up the phone
We've spent half the night arguing
Because you're there and I'm here
But what else can we do
I guess this is growing up
When things don't work out
And you fight to hold on
Until you realize that sometimes
The only thing you have
Is to keep moving on

It feels like the universe closes in around us when you touch me. But the moment is so fleeting and you are gone again. Then it is just me with too much space. The universe is awfully large, and I am awfully small, and I wish you were here to close the space.

There is so much noise
The city never sleeps
And I long for just one day everything is so
quiet
You and I could hear the clouds move

It's midnight and I thought about
Boarding a plane and meeting you in the city
I thought about stitching you into my skin
So you'd be with me as I slept
I wish you were here
Or I were there
Because my heart caves in when I look at you
And it feels like your hands twist around
My rib cage
And take the air from my lungs
My head starts pounding
And I just want to kiss you
It's midnight
And I just want you

I will love you through all the miles and the thoughts late at night.
I will love you through every day and as the darkness turns to light.
It's four o'clock in the afternoon and this is the hardest part.
But this is the way I love you, even if most days we are apart.

You take up all the space in my heart
and when you are not here,
I am jealous of the sheets that hold you,
because I am kept awake by the distance that keeps us apart.
But when I am with you,
I can barely express how much I care.
So let's just stay in bed all day
and I'll play with your hair.
We can share every innocent dream and talk about all our fears
and I will run my hands across your thighs and your hips.
I will kiss your forehead, your knuckles, and your lips.
Just tell me softly that you love me,
because when you said my name,
I swear my heart was never the same.

Wait for me;
I am coming home.
Wait for me;
You are the soul
I have always known.

Chicago

I'm in Chicago and you're at home;
how can we be so in love and yet so alone?
It's been so hard; how many more days must we be apart?
All the nerves in my heart, wondering if things have changed;
All the time apart, wondering if we'll still be the same.
I'm in Chicago and you're at home, and I'm watching life pass.
I miss you when I am alone.

Before the river takes our love and carries it out to sea,
I wanted to thank you for loving someone as broken as me.
I know it wasn't easy;
I know it wore you down.
Before the cities burn to ashes and the sky rains tears,
I wanted to say I'm sorry for all these wasted years.
Before our bones are no more our bones
and our lips are no longer our lips,
I hope you take a lover who sails a different ship.
May your nights become less brutal
and your mornings a little kinder;
May your heart find warmth with someone older
and a little wiser.

I've made a funny little habit of parking out near the bay. I like to watch the planes take off, fly overhead, and disappear into the clouds. I pretend I am up there too, on my way to see you.

Here is to tomorrow, bringing us one day closer to each other, until the day arrives that we meet again. Midnight weighs heavy on my soul as the earth folds into itself, every fold bringing us closer together.

And in the end it all matters, this distance that we are, creating all this longing.

The butterflies I feel for you, listening to our song on the radio, the way I miss you even in the early hours of the morning.

Wondering about the day I will have you through the night before.

The words are melting in my mouth like snow and I feel like I'm running on empty, but there are only seventeen more days until you're home. I have dreamt every night of the morning we are together again. You will be drinking coffee and I will be talking about how the leaves are changing. In your absence I can barely speak a word, but soon you will be home, and I will watch the leaves until we are together again.

But your love is not with you, not tomorrow, or the day after, or the next. So you find your lover in your dreams, and this is why you are always smiling in the dark, right before you sleep.

Time is valuable. For all the time we've lost by not being together, it has made you the most valuable thing to me.

But life has plans for all people. Even if those plans separate us from the ones we love. No matter where my life takes me or yours takes you, I will love you whether there are a thousand miles between us or none at all.

The distance isn't going to be easy. No one wants to sleep in an empty bed while you think about the one you love sleeping in theirs. Long-distance relationships are difficult, but they can also be beautiful. Imagine building a foundation of love, trust, and honesty without even a single touch. Then imagine the foundation when the snow finally returns to the mountain.

If you need encouragement

I will not bandage all your
Wounds
I will not kiss all your
Bruises
I will not admire all your
Scars
Instead I will watch you
As you bandage yourself
And mend all your bruises
And wear your own scars
Because you are your own
Hero
And all your sadness is
Yours
And I will love you
Because of it
All

She's that girl
who doesn't believe
in herself all that
much
and for the life of me
I can't understand
why
because my belief
in her
goes beyond the sky

I think about people sometimes
Like how they have their coffee
And if they like butter on their toast
I think about whether they're
Afraid of the same things I am
And whether they're chasing
Dreams every day
I think about the scars they
Have on their bodies
And the light that shines in their eyes
I think about whether they
Wear socks to bed
Or whether they have
Special-occasion clothes
Hanging in their closets
So if you're ever wondering
If someone thinks about you
From time to time
Then maybe this is your answer
I think about you a lot
I wonder if anyone is thinking about me too

But what is involved in a happily ever after? There are too many versions, not for you to choose but to create.

I know you feel like your best
Wasn't enough
I know you feel like all the hours
Were wasted
I know you feel disappointed
In yourself
But even though you feel
These things
Probably all at once right now
I just want you to know
That you're more than what
You believe
I look at you
And I know that you're
Smart
And beautiful
And capable
I believe in you
And I'll tell you every day
Until you believe it too

emotional and messy
sometimes lost and confused
but if you only realized
the wisdom behind those eyes
with a heart that never lies
would you storm the world
like you haven't a thing to lose?

and I know you're
a little insecure
and you think
just a little too much
but for all the times
you think you're
not what someone
needs
I'm thinking that
you are

You are a collection of miracles, bound together by sunlight. But you are also much more than that; you are a story, a home, a wolf that howls in the night.

Your feelings are valid and real. Do not let anybody denounce them just because they do not feel the same way. These feelings do not make you weak, or clingy, or overly emotional. They make you strong, brave, and beautiful. You are not merely made of stardust; you are the comet streaking through the sky on the way to do good and bright things.

There were many occasions when placing an out-of-order sign across your heart seemed the wisest decision to make. Only you didn't. Instead you kept your heart open, invited people in. And even when they were reckless, messy, and selfish, you chose to remain open: a shift that never ends, a light that always stays on, a beacon in the darkest night, a melody that carries on. I am in awe of you: an open prairie among an ever-changing cycle of wind.

The days will not stop; they will come for you. As easily as the moon lights the night sky and the sun rises, the days will come. So you must have courage, dear friend, courage in your heart to do all that must be done.

Maybe you're running scared because running is better than letting someone else in. But the truth is, you can't spend your whole life running. It's exhausting living in fear. Slow down. Chances and risks keep life interesting.

You're still here, you know;
under all the messy things,
under the stress, the anxiety, the sadness,
you're still you.
Come up for some air;
there are bright skies up here.
You have to pull yourself up;
I know you feel like you can't,
but you can.
I believe in you,
more than you know.

I do not see weakness in placing your heart on your sleeve; I see bravery in a world that can be cruel. I see something raw and beautiful in being as honest as you can be.

You just have to surround yourself with people who have the same heart as you.

But life is not about half doing. You cannot half love, or half accept, or half live. It's about giving everything you have. When you are old and worn, do you really want to look back and say you gave the bare minimum? You owe yourself more than that.

You can make all the effort in the world and yet someone will
still tell you it's not good enough.
But this isn't about them; it's about you.
You just need to be enough for you.

It's okay to close some doors; hell, it's even okay to lock them.

Let's be frank—there are times it feels the whole world is falling apart. You cannot compare your pain to others' so why respond with "Someone else has it worse?"

Pain is immeasurable when it's felt because in that moment it feels like the worst pain on earth.

Sometimes it's not even about calculations or careful thinking. Sometimes it's just about having a little faith that there are still people in the world who want only the best for you.

But you cannot grow if you are bitter.

Time has no agenda. You can meet someone and love them right away or grow your love over many years. You could have known someone for eternity and they still could not understand your core existence, yet the stranger at the bus stop knows exactly who you are. Time doesn't mean a thing.

Of all the important things you must do today, there is none greater than showing kindness to your heart. For even the brightest make mistakes and the wisest do not have a thing to say. Be gentle with yourself, forgive yourself, even on your darkest day.

Change is not going to sit you down and ask if you are ready. Change is not going to knock on your door and hand you notice. Change is not going to hug you in the middle of the night and tell you it can wait. Change does not wait. Change doesn't care if you aren't ready. It will happen anyway. Change is not always the friend you may want, but it will always know when you need it.

It's like Batman, basically.

If you are soul-searching

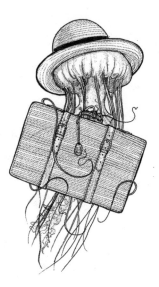

You are a battlefield. Never will there be a greater war than the one you hold with yourself.

be easy now
take some time
to clear the rubble
in your head
and teach your heart
that some things
are better left unsaid
don't worry
if sometimes things break
and change and burn
because these are things
to help you learn
and I know they're still
a part of you
inked into your skin
like a damaged tattoo
just don't forget
to love yourself too

This sky I look to with birds flying in opposite directions, with a mountain gaze cast downward, with land chopped up in tiny sections. There are too many ways to feel alone and not enough places to fall in love. Don't you understand? I dreamed of love and it gave me too many sleepless nights. And now sometimes I reach so far into the sky I wake up and I am not even in my bed.

Twenty-three

One day you wake up and you're twenty-three and you can't remember what it feels like to be seventeen but you still cry to your mother after a bad day and you look a little older but you don't really feel it. One day you're twenty-three and your great-aunt is telling you how mature you look and how you grew a little taller but inside you still remember sitting under the oak tree reading with no meetings tomorrow and no rent to pay and the only thing you can think about is how at seventeen you thought at twenty-three you would know everything and now you can't remember how you got from there to here. But seventeen-year-old you was wrong because you know only some things and not everything.

You know that coffee tastes better in the mornings and your home isn't your home anymore; it's "Mum and Dad's." You know your car needs servicing every six months and groceries are harder to do after breakups. She liked cookie dough and walnuts and strawberry-flavored milk and now every time you go to the store you can't buy spaghetti without remembering it was a Friday night and she kissed you for the first time and the heat from her skin could have set your entire place on fire. One day you're twenty-three and you're trying to explain to a seventeen-year-old all the mistakes you made so they won't make them too, when all you really want is for someone to realize you still don't have the first clue.

I feel as though I am always writing my first draft. As though my life is a series of edits that I never have time to complete.

But I am so deeply lost in my own soul, how can I expect anyone else to understand me?

Why are all the flowers gone?
I have looked for them everywhere
In the garden and along the street
In my bedroom and behind Grandma's chair
But the flowers are nowhere to be seen
Why are all the flowers gone?
Have we done something wrong?
Do we no longer act on what we mean?
Do we no longer care enough
To write about flowers in our songs?
Why are all the flowers gone?

Does art make sense to you? You are so brave and quiet; I think you would understand.

Stop acting like you aren't enough. You're strong and beautiful and the way you dress or who you like doesn't change how big your heart is.

You are important, and your hair looks nice, and so do your eyes,

and the way you eat half a tub of ice cream is sexy as hell.

You are not nothing, and you can achieve anything, and you are believed in.

You are someone worth having around and whoever has you now,

or will have you, is the lucky one too.

Why do people tell others what they deserve but never themselves?

Stop acting like you aren't enough, because you are.

Favorite Sweater

Sometimes you are someone's favorite sweater. They wear you all the time. They wear you around the house, out to dinner, to the movies, or even while they sleep. They wear you in front of their friends, and their families, and in front of strangers, because you are their favorite sweater and they want everyone to know. As it happens, whether on purpose or by accident, one day they hang you in the back of their closet. Before long, other sweaters are placed before you, and you watch them as they come and go, wondering if you'll ever be worn again. Soon you become not as accessible. The other sweaters are easily seen, and touched, and worn. You suddenly become far away. Far away means they forget the color in your eyes, and the way you smell, and your voice in the morning. So you hang, collecting dust and watching other sweaters keep the body you love warm. Maybe one day you'll be pulled from the closet, and they'll remember how they never felt as warm from all the other sweaters as they did with you. They'll remember how you promised not to scratch their skin or be stained with lies, and you kept those promises. But as it happens, maybe you were just a sweater, and you were only ever meant to be worn until they no longer needed you.

You've become so damaged
That when someone
Wants to give you
What you deserve
You have no idea
How to respond

There are always too many words to describe the way you are feeling. So why, then, when it comes time to say these words, do we lose them?

If you are in love and withering, then this is not love, because when in love, a rose should bloom.

Some things will never be fair for everyone. This is the saddest realization that the universe can teach. So if they are fair for you, remember to be grateful.

When you have been someone your whole life and suddenly you realize a part of you exists that you never realized before, it's perhaps the hardest thing to walk away from the you that you have always known. To walk into the open arms of this new, redefined you is like saying, I don't know you very well, but I want to.

Then I am reminded that life will continue on, regardless of whether I choose to board the train or stay on the platform.

They always say that transitions happen with big events. Like a wedding, your birthday, or your graduation. But maybe it's really in the smaller moments, like when you look at yourself in the mirror and realize how far you've come or how far you still have to go.

But a bed is much more than a place to sleep.
A carnival of dreams
A playground of growth
A haven in the dark
Warmth in the winter
Restless nights in the summer.
So when you invite someone to lie with you,
you are inviting them to your safe place.
Choose wisely.

Dear Life, you are exhausting at times. You throw more tantrums than I have ever known possible. You slow down, you speed up, you take time and give time. Sometimes there is sunshine and other times there are storms. So I try to break it up a little, take risks, love a lot, and find comfort in trying new things. But you are never the same, Life, always changing, always keeping me guessing. So I will live you, Life, to my absolute potential.

They don't teach you that some people will turn on you even after you have loved them with all the atoms in your body.
They don't teach you that some days you might not believe the sun will rise, but it will.
People hurt like you.
If you are heartbroken, the girl at the cashier or the boy on the train might be too.
You are not alone.
Just be kind.
Teach yourself.

We are all born with softness, and it's important to grow into it. Do not let the world turn your heart cold.

It's so hard to know what to say
To someone who feels so lost,
So I'll stand here for you
In the wind and the rain
And I'll be the lighthouse you need.
Take my hand and breathe again
And I will guide you home.

That's the thing about people who are soft. Everyone else thinks they can walk all over them as though they won't notice. But we do; we notice everything.

We are built on a foundation
Of what love is supposed to be
But today I need to tell you something
About who I am and who I am meant to be
And I know you might feel angry
Or maybe even sad
But just remember the day I was born
You promised to always love me
This is no longer a war I wish to wage
Between my head and my heart
I need to come out
And break free of this cage
Sometimes I am a rainstorm
Sometimes I am a drought
There is no in between
And I'm begging you to notice
I'm begging you to care
Because if I have to keep on hiding
Then life becomes unfair

We get older and suddenly what we cannot have becomes just what is. Less becomes plenty and time is a fragment of our short adventure on earth.

You will always be a lot of things.
Not everyone is going to like you or understand you.
And in the times it feels like you are on trial,
Try to treat others with good intentions,
Even the ones that don't deserve it.
Be you, even when it's hard.

If you need a reason to stay

These words aren't going to change the world, but maybe they will make you think twice about changing yours.

Here are some nice things: warm nights after the rain, old books, new books, tea in the afternoon, snow angels, palm trees, smiling, laughing, hugs that make you feel like you are combusting, wet-nosed kisses from your dog, waterfalls, sunsets, a clear night sky, the hopes and dreams of you and me. A kitten curled in your lap, fresh laundry, favorite songs, the morning birds in perfect harmony. Nice simple things to remind you to stay.

And I promise your heart will go on, as damaged as you think it may seem. I can tell you that you will be okay, the most okay that anyone has seen.

There you are
With all your little
Inconsistencies
And all your little
Flaws
You push people
Away
Because it's easier
Simpler
Secrets in your veins
Hidden years in your
Eyes
Please don't be
Afraid
I know what you are
It's written under your skin
Three little words
You mean everything

By existing you are planting softness in soil that has turned hard. There is no need to surrender your existence. You are doing just fine by even existing at all.

Some days you are raw
and things are falling apart
and when you look in the mirror,
you see an enemy,
someone you hate with all your heart,
but this is not how they see you.
When they look back at you,
they see an entire universe;
you are a body of art,
you are a map of galaxies,
you are every flower,
lovely from the start.
So when recovery seems far away
and no one understands,
when life cannot get any worse
and you would rather cry all day,
know you are wanted and loved.
I cannot survive.
Yes, you can.
You are needed,
so please
choose to stay alive.

Gentle Reminders

I have come to know that it is better to feel
than to feel nothing at all.
Conversations are meant to be honest,
even when your stomach is in knots
and you cannot speak.
You can be in love at 3 a.m. or 5 p.m.
and sometimes it is with someone else
and other times it is with the way the sky looks
on a Saturday afternoon.
You will make hard decisions and easy decisions,
but they are all important.
Appreciate those little moments on the beach
with a beer and a good sunset.
I'm so sorry for anyone who has ever hurt you,
but please don't close your heart to love.
You need love, and love needs you.
You are the sun, and the moon, and every star
and you deserve someone who will cross the universe for you.
Forgive, even if you are angry.
Forgive, even if they broke all their promises to you.
Say it: I forgive you.
You don't even realize how beautiful you are, do you?
If I could tell you this every day, for the rest of your life,
I would.
Even if I do not know your name and we never meet,
you are beautiful.

You can be miles apart,
but this will never measure the way you feel
when your best friend says exactly what you need to hear.
Don't stay bitter for too long. Learn, move on, and grow.
Remember to try and try again.
If someone makes you nervous, you probably make them
nervous too.
Why do you always think you are bothering someone?
Stop that.
Do not change your inner values and who you truly are for
anyone.
Validation on the Internet can be a dangerous thing;
try to stay humble.
If someone does not appreciate your story or cherish you,
this does not mean that someone else won't.
You will find them one day.
They are probably wondering when they will find you, too.
Life can be chaotic and sometimes people will hurt you,
but in the middle of all your loud thoughts and sleepless nights,
just remember that magic grows in flowers,
the sun can make your heart race after the rain,
and whenever you can make someone smile,
you will forget all the reasons you were ever sad.

Make a list.
Write down the most important things.
I will give you the first:
You.

Some days will always be harder than others. Be patient with yourself; you have won many battles but the war will take time. You can be seventeen or seventy-eight and still make mistakes. Try not to punish yourself too much over them. You will compare yourself to others, everyone does it, but try to remember someone compares themselves to you, too. Be kinder to the thoughts in your head; you are thinking them for a reason. There will always be that person who you gave your whole heart to and it still wasn't enough for them. But you will always be enough for yourself. And when all's said and done, that's the person who lives your life.

That's the person you have to impress.

Be a friend to yourself, not an enemy.

The earth has a heart and you exist somewhere inside, so if you need a reason to stay, take a moment, a deep breath; don't go breaking the earth's heart now.

Trust that your body is a castle, and no matter how many wars are waged at its front gates, your castle will always remain standing.

It makes me sad, truly, that you were made to feel as though you were annoying or stupid or that you aren't beautiful when you talk about the things you love or that you aren't interesting at 7 p.m. or 5 a.m. Your existence is important. You are important.

The Bricklayer

Once I met a bricklayer on a sunny afternoon
I had only just surfaced from my deep slumber underneath the
moon
I asked him why he was building such a wall
But he did not respond and I wondered if he'd heard me at all
He worked until the sun dipped low to touch the skyline
Building his wall higher, I'd never seen such a design
"Sir," I called, but he was behind the wall
"Sir," I called again, but the wall was far too tall
And then came a faint sound I barely heard
"This is what you wanted, what you preferred!"
But I looked at the wall looming above
A wall keeping everything out
Even love

Be kind to yourself, the way you would be to someone you love.

You weren't always like this, were you? Once vibrant and full of life, and all it takes is too many lies, a handful of betrayals, and a bucket full of hurt, and now suddenly you are wondering how someone could have been so cruel to damage your garden. So today, cover all those lies in soil, plant daisies, and watch them sprout and breathe life. Take a handful of forgiveness and scatter this around too, and then pour a bucket of happiness for good measure. Now take a moment, allow your new garden to grow, heal yourself, and bring yourself back to the life you have always known.

Even on bad days and cold nights where it feels it has all but gone. You still have purpose. It has been inside you since the day you were born. A tiny little firefly born from the light of the universe. There is a world of reason inside you, an entire library of thoughts and emotions. For all the moments that steal your hope, just remember the universe intended for you to happen. You have purpose.

Things might not get better tomorrow. You may have many tomorrows and nothing changes. But that is not the point. The point of moving through all these tomorrows is to get to the one tomorrow that finally does get better.

Throw down Your Scissors

Throw down your scissors; your skin is much too strong
Throw down your scissors; even when tears flow all night long
Throw down your scissors; there are other ways to let the light
in
Throw down your scissors; let your faith seep deep into your
skin
Throw down your scissors; you are loved in every way
Throw down your scissors; stay here with us
and fight another day

I am sure they will make the road to recovery seem clean. They'll use words to make healing seem pretty and pretend the bandages don't feel heavy and still cause pain. Your sadness is never going to be neat and tidy, and on some days you might even wonder how you're possibly going to pick up every shattered piece on the floor when burying your soul seems much easier. There will be moments where you have to convince yourself that feeling is better than being numb and that your aching bones are strong enough to carry on. There will be times things feel upside down and you are spinning on an axis that is never balanced. There will be days where you take steps backward and those new steps forward feel very far away. But even in the difficulty you are still taking steps; you are still making progress. And for every bump along the way, just remember you have come this far; might as well keep going.

You will always be somebody to someone else. You will always need other people. And coffee, you will always need good coffee too.

Of course there will be moments when you feel as though you are completely out of options. But there will be one option to always start with: forgive yourself.

There is always going to be chaos. Humans are made to be messy. Yet even in the hurricane there is a calm that will radiate. It spreads after any disaster, and the pieces are picked back up again.

There is a great deal of difficulty
in surviving
And it starts with choosing to feel
the good
and especially the bad

You'll end up surprising yourself, you know. Like how strong you are and how much your heart can grow. One minute you're in pieces and broken on the floor and the next you're putting on your shoes and heading out the door. Remember all those that smiled at you and who told you to have a good day. They are the little gifts sent to you reminding you to stay.

These are for you

Describe her, they said. So I tried to think of all the things I could say about you. Like the color of your hair and the freckles across your back. How you collect notebooks in your spare time and the way you sound in the morning. From your lips, your curves, and your thighs to the generosity in your heart and the fire in your eyes. But when I think about it, I couldn't quite describe you the way you deserve to be described. Because in the moments you look at me, I love you more than I will ever be able to epitomize.

I'm living a life where things are temporary,
but with you,
all my walls have caved in
and I know that you are worth it;
you are anything but ordinary.
For every time you murmur my name,
take my hand, and run your lips over mine,
you should know I am falling ever harder.
And when you look at me with those eyes,
I know inside you are falling just the same.
So beautiful girl, come as you are
with every stitch and every scar.
I have found everything in you;
I'm so crazy in love with you.

I can't remember what it was like not to know you. I am not sure if this is because we have met before. As though we have seen each other in a different time and life and maybe your soul is the one soul I keep running into. Or maybe it's just because my life before you wasn't nearly as exciting. All I know is when we met, we spent the afternoon in front of a beautiful view, and yet all I could do was look at you.

She has hair that reminds me of the sun. Sometimes when I kiss her, it feels like the earth is moving and I am moving with it. She has green eyes that are sometimes light and sometimes dark depending on the time of day. She smiles like she knows what you are thinking. Her skin feels soft but rough across the tops of her hands. Her fingers knot through mine in the middle of the night. She smells like dusk after a thunderstorm and I am not sure how she looks so beautiful in the mornings, but she does. She has freckles in places that make her body look like the sky and they are her stars, and even if my soul knew hers in a thousand different lifetimes, I am sure I would fall in love with her in each one.

Just listen to her. Listen to her heart, her mind, her body, and her soul. And if you are lucky enough to find a soul that is beautiful, make sure you tell her.

I wish that I could give you more
Because that's what you deserve
While I'm sailing around the world
Please always know
That you are who I call home
If you were to ever leave
I am not sure what I would do
Because you are all I need

This is my life
and I will fall for you every day
because you are my love
and I see you in everything.

There may come times when things just seem hard
and you're running on empty,
walking through days blind.
There may come moments when things seem too much,
like you keep coming up last,
and you're losing your touch.
But you are my life, and I'll spend every single day
reminding you that you are capable,
you are smart and strong,
and you will find your way.
Hearts can hurt, minds can ache,
the world may seem far too big,
and everything feels at stake.
But you will reach your dreams
no matter how difficult it seems,
and I will always believe in you,
in all that you ever set out to do.

Our skin will only be young once. All the moments we spend naked under the sheets, passion running high and blood pumping through our veins, will be memories. But forty years from now, you'll still make my heart race when your hand touches mine, and my passion will always be you.

It will be dawn soon. The sun will rise and the grass will cough in the morning dew. And I am excited, stirring from my sleep, because in the early light, I get to look at you.

I wish there were a better way to tell you how much I love you. To write it in the sky or dip all my feelings in gold. But the truth is, it's much simpler than all of those things. All I know is that I wake up each morning and I can never find the words to explain how much I feel for you.

Something in the way you wore your hair that night, or maybe it was the dress you had on and how it fit all your curves in all the right places. And while I was busy trying not to stare, you were ordering coffee, and the shape of your lips and even the way you spoke were enough to knock me out.

Here I am after all this time, hopelessly and madly in love with you.

Perhaps I am old fashioned, but when I think of you and me, I think of a house in the suburbs with nothing but warmth inside, and I think of spending all my days taking care of you and facing every challenge together in life's ever-changing tide.

Sometimes when I'm coming home, she'll wait by the door and kiss me under the fading light of the day. She'll say it's because she forgot to leave the key out, but when she looks at me, I know it is because I am loved. There was a time before we had met and all my stars had burned out, until one day she found me and suddenly there was no longer any doubt. There she was with a smile in the early morning and I was in love again. I dream with her about the house we will have and all our days growing old. Someday when our skin is worn and our hair is gray, I will still look at her like she is the sun on a rainy day. I will never say I'm sorry for the way I feel about her, because she is all I need. And every single time I look at her, I know we'll make it anywhere. She is honest and true and fair and my heart belongs to her with every memory we share. Even if she never understands why she means so much, I will spend all my days falling more in love with her.

I am flooded with your absence. I drown in how much I miss you. How do you enrage a storm of loneliness inside me? In the afternoon, I walk across fields of flowers and I see young couples together and in love. I declare my love for you to the poppies and ask them to bring you home, and in the night I long for you and write these sad little poems.

We forget things.

Wallets, keys, days of the week.

Sometimes we forget important things.

Birthdays, anniversaries, meetings.

But I will never forget my love for you.

It has settled in my mind so deeply I dream of you every night.

It has wound so tightly around my heart it beats to the sound of your name. It has nestled forever in my lungs; I breathe you in and out.

I forget things, but never you.

It seems silly what your name does to me. I love the way it looks on a card I have scrawled for your birthday. I love the way it looks in a letter I have scribbled in my car. I love the way it looks when it lights up my phone. I love the way it sounds when asked if you will be there too. Perhaps I will meet others with the same name, but none will ring so loudly in my heart as it does when they are speaking about you.

Sometimes when she is sleeping, I think about waking her up. I know that this is selfish but I crave the sound of her voice.

Sometimes when she is talking, I interrupt to kiss her. I know that this is selfish but I crave the taste of her lips.

Sometimes when she is not looking, I steal her sweaters. I know that this is selfish but I crave the way she smells.

Sometimes I hold her face in my hands so she cannot pull away. I know that this is selfish but I crave the way she looks at me.

Sometimes when we are driving, I will take the long way home. I know that this is selfish but I crave the touch of her hand in mine.

Sometimes I cannot control the patterns of my thoughts or the aching in my chest, because I crave her always. I crave her everything.

That's the best part, when the sun dips low in the afternoon and I get to lie down with you and tell you all about my day. It won't matter how you're dressed or how you look. It won't matter the things we can afford or the parties we get invited to. I just care that you listen, even if sometimes you are listening for hours.

My heart has never been very sensible.
I've been lost in cities
and torn apart.
I've been distracted, burning bright
with reckless reactions.
But please believe me when I say
you are the best decision
I have ever made.

The small things still give me butterflies. Like the way you say I love you without even saying it. When you call me to let me know you are bringing the wine for dinner. When I am half asleep in the early morning and you pull the covers over my shoulders as you leave for work. When I shower and I notice you have placed all your little shampoos on my shelf. There are pieces of you all around my house, your clothes in my drawer, your empty coffee cups on my desk, and your jewelry on the table. I have always thought that love was about big moments, that I had to endure pain because love was worth it. Yet here you are, and our love is just simple, pure, a love that I want for the rest of our lives.

Looking for Ice Cream

We were in the grocery store. You wanted ice cream even though it was cold out. You couldn't decide which flavor and I was teasing you about being so indecisive sometimes. I suggested we just buy every flavor in the store and you laughed. It was the kind of laugh I could listen to for the rest of my life. You said I was silly and you kissed me, pressed against me so I could feel how cold the tip of your nose was. You were only in sweats, hair so messy from being in bed all afternoon. And in that moment I knew I loved you more than anyone else I had ever loved. In that moment I knew you were my once in a lifetime. And yet all we were doing was looking for ice cream.

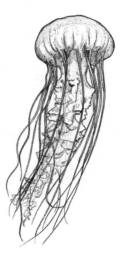

Thank you for reading this book. I hope you enjoyed
reading it as much as I enjoyed writing it.
You can view more of my work on Twitter
@CourtPeppernell and Instagram @itsonlyyforever

Feel free to write to me via courtney@pepperbooks.org

Pillow Thoughts

Andrews McMeel Publishing
a division of Andrews McMeel Universal
1130 Walnut Street, Kansas City, Missouri 64106

www.andrewsmcmeel.com

Illustrations by Ryan Gerber

18 19 20 21 22 BVG 10 9 8 7

ISBN: 978-1-4494-8975-5

Library of Congress Control Number: 2017941958

Editor: Patty Rice
Art Director, Designer: Diane Marsh
Production Editor: Mariah Marsden
Production Manager: Cliff Koehler

ATTENTION: SCHOOLS AND BUSINESSES
Andrews McMeel books are available at quantity
discounts with bulk purchase for educational, business,
or sales promotional use. For information, please
e-mail the Andrews McMeel Publishing Special Sales
Department: specialsales@amuniversal.com.